A Guide for Using

The Enormous Egg

in the Classroom

Based on the novel written by Oliver Butterworth

This guide written by **Lorraine Kujawa**

Teacher Created Materials, Inc.
6421 Industry Way
Westminster, CA 92683
www.teachercreated.com
©*2000 Teacher Created Materials, Inc.*
Made in U.S.A.
ISBN 1-57690-632-9

Edited by
Gisela Lee

Illustrated by
Bruce Hedges

Cover Art by
Wendy Chang

Table of Contents

Introduction 3

Sample Lesson Plan 4

Before the Book *(Pre-reading Activities)* 5

About the Author 7

Book Summary 8

Vocabulary List 9

Vocabulary Activity Ideas 10

Section 1 *(Chapters 1–3)* 11

- Quiz Time!
- Cooperative Learning Activity—How Much Would You Do?
- Curriculum Connection—Examination of Eggs
- Hands-on Project—Exactly Eggs
- Into Your Life—Your Own Story

Section 2 *(Chapters 4–7)* 16

- Quiz Time!
- Hands-on Project—Dino Coloring Book
- Cooperative Learning Activity—Choices and Consequences
- Curriculum Connection—Call the Doctor!
- Into Your Life—Being a Caretaker

Section 3 *(Chapters 8–11)* 21

- Quiz Time!
- Hands-on Project—Biscuits for Breakfast
- Cooperative Learning Activity—You're Like That!
- Curriculum Connection—Place the Dinosaur
- Into Your Life—To Go Where You Have Never Gone Before

Section 4 *(Chapters 12–14)* 26

- Quiz Time!
- Hands-on Project—Be the Scientist
- Cooperative Learning Activity—A World of Schooling
- Curriculum Connection—Freedom, New Hampshire, to Washington, D.C.
- Into Your Life—Planning a Trip

Section 5 *(Chapters 15–17)* 31

- Quiz Time!
- Hands-on Project—Passing a Bill
- Curriculum Connection—How Congress Does It
- Cooperative Learning Activity—Speech! Speech!
- Into Your Life—A Political Letter

After the Book *(Post-reading Activities)*

- Any Questions? 36
- Book Report Ideas 37
- Research Activity—Scavenger Hunt 38

Culminating Activities 39

Unit Test Options 43

Bibliography of Related Reading 46

Answer Key 47

Introduction

A good book can become a good friend. It stimulates our imaginations, gives us information, and offers inspiration. A good book can keep us company. Each time we read a good book, we enter a world that gives us a new way of looking at things. Each new story stays with us forever. In *Literature Units* we select books that become our close friends.

Teachers using this unit will find the following features a great addition to their own valuable ideas:

- Sample Lesson Plan
- Pre-reading Activities
- Biographical Sketch of the Author
- Book Summary
- Vocabulary List and Vocabulary Activity Ideas
- Chapters grouped for study with sections that include the following:

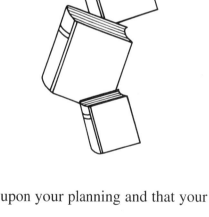

  —quizzes
  —hands-on projects
  —cooperative learning activities
  —cross-curriculum connections
  —extensions into the reader's own life

- Post-reading Activities
- Book Report Ideas
- Research Activity
- Culminating Activities
- Three Different Unit Test Options
- Bibliography of Related Reading
- Answer Key

We are confident that using this unit will be a positive influence upon your planning and that your students will be enriched by the stories you present to them.

Sample Lesson Plan

Lesson 1

- Introduce and complete some or all of the pre-reading activities located on page 5.
- Create your egg activity on page 6.
- Read "About the Author" with students (page 7).
- Introduce the vocabulary list for Section 1 (page 9).

Lesson 2

- Read chapters 1 through 3. While you read, place the vocabulary words in the context of the story and discuss their meanings.
- Do a vocabulary activity (page 10).
- Work on "How Much Would You Do?" (page 12).
- Do an "Examination of Eggs" (page 13).
- Work on "Exactly Eggs" (page 14).
- Complete "Your Own Story" on page 15.
- Administer the Section 1 quiz (page 11).
- Introduce the vocabulary list for Section 2 (page 9).

Lesson 3

- Read chapters 4 through 7. Place vocabulary words in context and discuss their meanings.
- Do a vocabulary activity (page 10).
- Make a "Dino Coloring Book" (page 17).
- Complete "Choices and Consequences" (page 18).
- Find out how to "Call the Doctor!" (page 19).
- Consider "Being A Caretaker" (page 20).
- Administer the Section 2 quiz (page 16).
- Introduce the vocabulary list for Section 3 (page 9).

Lesson 4

- Read chapters 8 through 11. Place the vocabulary words in context and discuss their meanings.
- Do a vocabulary activity (page 10).
- Make "Biscuits for Breakfast" (page 22).
- Discover how "You're Like That!" (page 23).
- Decide where to place the dinosaurs (page 24).

- Consider some new places to see (page 25).
- Administer the Section 3 quiz (page 21).
- Introduce the vocabulary list for Section 4 (page 9).

Lesson 5

- Read chapters 12 through 14. Place the vocabulary words in context and discuss their meanings.
- Do a vocabulary activity (page 10).
- Become a scientist (page 27).
- Discover "A World of Schooling" (page 28).
- Follow the trail from Freedom, New Hampshire, to Washington, D.C. (page 29).
- Plan your own trip (page 30).
- Administer the Section 4 quiz (page 26).
- Introduce the vocabulary list for Section 5 (page 9).

Lesson 6

- Read chapters 15 through 17. Place the vocabulary words in context and discuss their meanings.
- Do a vocabulary activity (page 10).
- Create your own laws (page 32).
- See how the government makes a law (page 33).
- Make your own speech (page 34).
- Write a political letter (page 35).
- Administer the Section 5 quiz (page 31).

Lesson 7

- Discuss any questions your students have about the story (page 36).
- Assign a book report and a research activity (pages 37 and 38).
- Begin work on one or more of the culminating activities (pages 39–42).

Lesson 8

- Administer the Unit Test: 1, 2, and/or 3 (pages 43–45).
- Discuss test answers and possible corrections.
- Provide a list of related reading for students (page 46).

Before the Book

Before you begin reading *The Enormous Egg* with your students, work on a pre-reading activity to encourage interest and enhance comprehension of their reading. Here are some suggestions that might work for your class.

1. Look over the book and reflect on these questions:
   - How does the cover suggest what might be the main issue in the story?
   - In what way does the title suggest that something unusual will occur in the book?
   - What must an author do to keep his or her audience interested in reading the story?
   - Why do you think this book is divided into chapters instead of being one long story?
   - How can being responsible for something change a person's life?
   - What are some important factors that make a family a happy one?
   - Does being responsible for a pet make life harder or more enjoyable?

2. Being responsible means being accountable for something within one's power. Brainstorm ideas of ways people are responsible. What does it mean to you to be responsible?

3. What kinds of choices do people make that change their lives? Discuss choices with the class.

4. On page 6 there are outlines of various eggs. Assign students to research one of the animals represented. Locate and record information about the size of the egg, weight, time for gestation (how long it takes to hatch), who takes care of the egg before it hatches, how the egg is stored, and any other interesting information. Cut out the pattern of the assigned egg and trace around it on white poster board. Cut out the poster board egg, and use a portion of clay to stand it up for a display. Have students report on their eggs when their research is done.

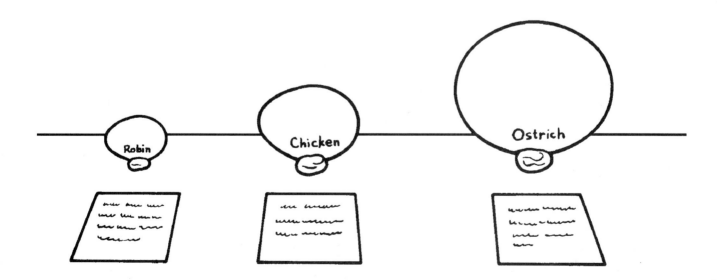

Before the Book *(cont.)*

Egg Outlines

Since *The Enormous Egg* deals with an unusual egg, it might be interesting to see what some usual eggs are like. Use the outlines below to help you study some facts about eggs.

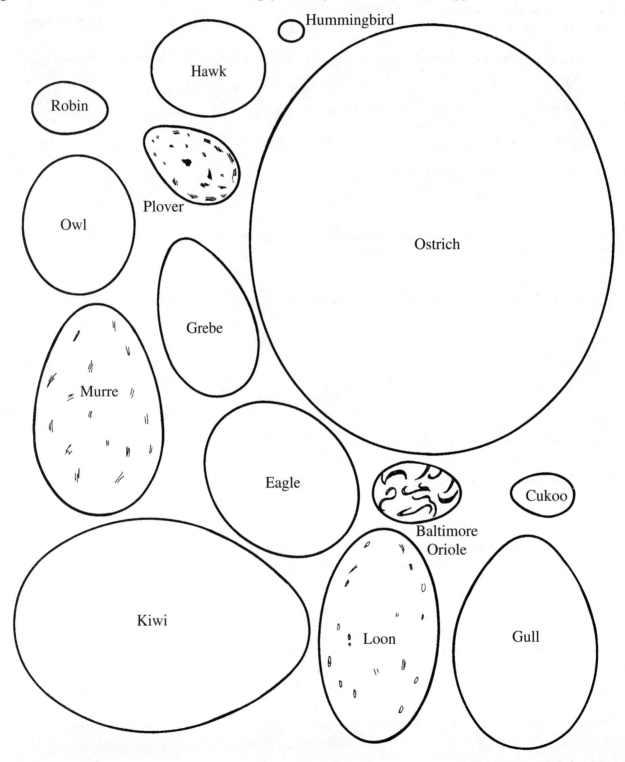

About the Author

Oliver Butterworth was born in Hartford, Connecticut, on May 23, 1915. He lived until 1990; he was 75 years old when he died. He was married to Marian Brooks in 1940 and had four children: Michael, Timothy, Dan, and Kate.

Butterworth attended Dartmouth College and went to graduate school at Harvard and Middlebury College.

He liked camping, traveling, and mountain climbing and was an educator as well as an author of children's books.

He wrote *The Enormous Egg* in 1956. He also wrote *The Trouble with Jenny's Ears, The Narrow Passage, A Visit to the Big House,* and *Orrie's Run.*

"I began writing for children after I had taught two years in elementary school," Butterworth explained. At the time he wrote his first book, at age 40, it was thought that the repetition of words was the way to learn reading. Sentences like "Look, look Jane" were common.

"I thought if I could write a book that sounded like a twelve-year-old talking," he said, "then children would like it. It seemed to work. It came as a great surprise." Butterworth considered writing for children "like talking to yourself and keeping one ear cocked to children, listening to their concerns."

The Enormous Egg quickly became a classic in children's literature. The central story came from an experience with his own chickens and also was a response to a political problem that arose in the 1950s. At that time, Senator Joseph McCarthy was on a search for Communists in the United States. Many innocent people were falsely accused, and many lives were ruined because of McCarthy's accusations. "I saw him as a bully," said Oliver Butterworth. "He was throwing his weight around—getting teachers and books thrown out of schools. It finally occurred to me that I had no way to confront him except to write about him. I think of books as a message to write to people, as well as forms of entertainment, and try to keep a sort of balance between the fun and the more serious purpose."

The Twentieth Century Children's Writers organization writes that Butterworth has earned a lasting place in the hearts of child readers because of his rare ability to recall the substance of childhood dreams of glory, finding treasures, making contact with the past, and keeping the adult population in place.

Butterworth wished to "tell children about what is precious to me, about the colors of life, the green freedom of leaves and grass, the gray-blue of hills and streams, the bone-white color of honesty, the flesh tones of the warm pulse of families together . . . and the true-blue of courage to speak up for what you think is right."

The Enormous Egg

by Oliver Butterworth
(Houghton Mifflin, 1995)
(Available in Canada from Thomas Allen & Son, in UK from Cassell, and in AUS from Jackaranda Wiley)

The Enormous Egg takes place on a small farm in Freedom, New Hampshire. Nate Twichell is twelve and lives with his parents and his sister Cynthia. His father owns a newspaper in town called *The Freedom Sentinel*. They have a rooster named Ezekiel, some chickens, a goat, and a vegetable garden.

One day, Nate notices that one of the hens has become so large that she can hardly waddle. Soon after, the hen lays an enormous leathery egg. The large egg isn't what anyone expected. Dad considers having it for breakfast, but Mom won't have it in the house. So they decide to wait to see what hatches out of it.

Since the poor hen can't turn the great egg, Nate comes to the hen house several times a day to turn it for her. When the newspapers hear of the giant egg, people come to measure it, take pictures, and weigh it.

After six weeks, the egg finally hatches into an unusual creature with knobs sticking out of its head, a leathery collar, and a long tail like a lizard. Dr. Ziemer, a paleontologist, says it's a triceratops.

The first major problem with which the Twichell family is faced is the task of feeding the growing triceratops, now called Uncle Beasley. He seems to double in size every day. Crowds begin to gather about the Twichell family home. Dr. Kennedy, from the United States National Museum, makes an offer to buy Uncle Beasley. A gas station owner wants to put Uncle Beasley in front of his gas station to draw in customers. The Old Mill Pond Whiskey Corporation wants to rent him, and even a luggage company wants to use Uncle Beasley to make dinosaur luggage. Uncle Beasley keeps on growing.

When the summer is over, the family and Dr. Ziemer decide that Uncle Beasley should go to the National Museum in Washington and that Nate can stay with Uncle Beasley for four weeks. To exercise Uncle Beasley, Nate gets up early in the morning and walks him around the streets of Washington.

A slight mishap with a truck puts an end to their walks, and Uncle Beasley is moved to the Elephant House at the National Zoological Park.

A problem arises when Senator Granderson proposes a law to forbid a foreign animal to live in the United States. So Dr. Ziemer tells Nate to go on television and ask people to write to their congressmen. Nate tells the cameras what he knows about Uncle Beasley and encourages people to tell their senators and representatives to vote against the dinosaur bill. People pour out support for Nate's dinosaur. Thousands come to Washington to wave protest signs at the zoo and donate money to make sure the dinosaur bill is defeated.

When Nate goes home after his four weeks are up, he is met with a parade led by the school band.

In the latest letter sent to Nate from Dr. Ziemer, he learns that Uncle Beasley is now 20 feet long and weighs thirteen thousand nine hundred pounds—and he's still growing!

Nate's dad suggests that he write his story down in a book. If you are in Washington, D.C., at the Elephant House and see a boy in the dinosaur cage riding the dinosaur, that boy is Nathan Twichell.

Vocabulary List

Section 1
Chapters 1–3

almanac	sentinel	waddle
gunwale	mushmelon	teetering
fate	cove	specimens

Section 2
Chapters 4–7

ease	commotion	quivering	persuade	triplet
saucepan	fossil	paleontologist	trembling	triceratops
tremendously	enormous	inquisitive	hullabaloo	colleagues
brace	residence	squatted	accustomed	poisonous
reptiles	gizzard	skeletons	skeptic	buffoon

Section 3
Chapters 8–11

impatient	admirable	metabolism	proposition
jolt	bedlam	situation	remarkable
instant	glum	gladioli	nuisance
parlor	dubious	shuddered	ventilated
degenerate	eclipse	dismal	enthusiastic

Section 4
Chapters 12–14

gladiola	observation	potentially	notion
superintendent	designated	specimen	mincemeat
traipsing	brute	gawk	incident
hopper	swarming	patiently	alfalfa
ramp	tortoise	managed	marble

Section 5
Chapters 15–17

tradition	dissuade	corridor	tangled	whim
constitutes	various	dismay	grieve	squandering
absolutely	freakish	inefficient	outlandish	destiny
possession	exterminated	gluttonous	emphasize	surplus
quivery	gloomy	wrangled	logical	shivers
sashaying	descended	principles	delegation	ornament

Vocabulary Activity Ideas

❑ **Vocabulary Conversations**

Have laminated sets of words to give to students. When a student uses one of the words in conversation in a correct manner, the word card goes to the other person. It gets placed in a designated box in the room. Those using all of the words can each receive an award.

❑ **Vocabulary Comics**

Create a vocabulary comic sheet folded accordion style. Cut an 8 1/2" x 11" (22 cm x 28 cm) sheet of paper in half lengthwise. Fold in three-inch (8 cm) sections. In each section, print a vocabulary word at the bottom of that section and, using colored pencils, create a picture that represents the vocabulary word. Use as a reference when going over the words.

❑ **Poster or Bulletin Board**

Create a poster or bulletin board with pictures, drawn or cut out, representing each of the vocabulary words. Divide each word picture with a solid line to set it off. Have word cards placed separately on the board. Ask students to match words with pictures.

❑ **Spelling Bee**

Have a spelling bee with two teams. Have students line up along one wall and then measure out a number of steps that students will take as they play. When each student spells a word, that student can take a step forward. The student who reaches the end of the course first wins a point for his or her team. You could have a prize for the winning team and a second prize for the runner-up.

❑ **Vocabulary Charades**

Hand each student a card with a vocabulary word on it and have the student attempt to act out the word without speaking for two minutes. Students try to guess the word. The person who guesses the answer gets to act next.

❑ **Story Time**

Have students take 15 minutes to create an adventure story using several of their new vocabulary words. Give each student a piece of plastic and markers to fashion a picture for their story for the overhead projector. The student reads or tells the story using the new vocabulary words. Discuss with students ahead of time what is acceptable and not acceptable subject matter for a classroom story. Students may work in pairs.

❑ **Vocabulary Hats**

Roll up the ends of a paper bag to form a hat for each student. Leave a one-inch band around the hat, taping the ends together. Holding cards with vocabulary words on them, students circulate for ten minutes while wearing their hats. Each time a student uses a vocabulary word correctly in a sentence to another student, he or she gives up that card. The receiving student places it in the band of his or her hat. The goal is to give away all your original cards and collect as many new vocabulary cards as possible in your hat.

❑ **Vocabulary Bingo**

You will need place markers (buttons, corn, etc.) and a 5" x 5" (13 cm x 13 cm) card. Draw a 1" x 1" (2.54 cm x 2.54 cm) grid on each card. Place one vocabulary word neatly in each section. The teacher will call out the definition of each word, and the student will place a marker in the correct place. Use typical Bingo rules for winners. Provide a small prize for each win. Students may exchange cards.

Quiz Time!

Answer the following questions about Chapters 1–3 in complete sentences. You may use your book to find the answers.

1. Where did Nate get his enormous egg?

   _____

   _____

2. How could you tell that the Twichell family got along well?

   _____

   _____

3. Why did Ezekiel have to stay in the basement?

   _____

   _____

4. What did Pop mean when he said, "We may have the right to disturb the neighbors, but we'd better not disturb Mrs. Parsons . . . "?

   _____

   _____

5. What are some of the choices the Twichell family had to take care of the problem with Ezekiel and Mrs. Parsons?

   _____

   _____

6. Who took on the responsibility of turning the egg?

   _____

   _____

7. How did the Twichell family show they were reasonable people?

   _____

   _____

8. How did Dr. Ziemer meet Nate?

   _____

   _____

9. What did Dr. Ziemer mean by saying that the egg might hatch "into something of an unusual appearance"?

   _____

   _____

10. How would the story have evolved differently if Nate had broken the egg before it hatched?

   _____

   _____

How Much Would You Do?

Nate Twichell spent a great deal of time taking care of his unusual egg. He took time off from fishing, postponed a camping trip to Franconia Notch, and said that he would have done anything to see that egg hatch. Was having the egg hatch worth the effort? What would you be willing to do to have something that you wanted?

Working with a classmate, look up these words that have to do with achieving a goal. Write their meanings on the lines provided:

dedicated:_____

commit: _____

industry:_____

endeavor: _____

scheme:_____

determination: _____

toil: _____

succeed: _____

strategy: _____

effort: _____

elbow grease: _____

tenacious: _____

With your partner, decide on goals that a person your age might want to have. List them below and decide what you would be willing to do to achieve these goals.

Discuss your plans with the class, incorporating several of the words you defined above.

Goal	What has to be done? *(Be specific.)*

Examination of Eggs

Nate had the chance to gather eggs right from the hens in his back yard. Now's your chance to take a good look at eggs.

For this project you will need: one chicken egg, a small bowl, a light, a spoon, a paper towel, and a pencil.

As you follow the directions, working with a partner or by yourself, check off each instruction.

❑ Carefully hold the egg in the palm of your hand. Feel its weight and the hardness and texture of its shell. Hold it up to a light and see if you can see the air space in the fatter end of the egg.

❑ While you hold your egg over a small bowl, carefully crack the egg with a spoon and gently lay the inside of the egg in the bowl, being careful not to break the yolk. Examine the inside of the shell. See in what way the ends are different. Look carefully at the lining inside the shell.

❑ Observe how many sections of the clear liquid (albumen) surround the yolk. Can you find the germ spot where the chick can begin life?

❑ Locate the white strands on either side of the yolk that are used to hold it in the center of the egg.

❑ Using your spoon, gently lift out the yolk of the egg and notice the different consistency of the albumen.

❑ After placing the yolk back into the bowl, touch the yolk with your finger and observe how it is held together with a membrane.

❑ With the end of the spoon, carefully break the skin of the yolk. Notice what comes out of the yolk.

❑ When you are done examining the egg, clean your work area and wash your hands thoroughly with soap and water.

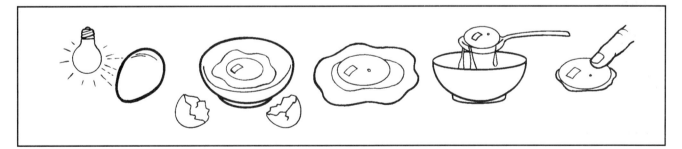

On the back of this sheet, make a list of everything you observed while investigating the egg. Feel free to share ideas no one else may have noticed.

Consider these questions to be discussed with your class. You may make up some questions of your own.

• What do you think happens to the yolk as the chick in the egg develops?

• Explain how the developing chick is provided the basics of life: food, air, and shelter.

• How would having a square egg change the ability of the egg to develop into a chick?

• Since bones are made of calcium and the shell of the egg is made of calcium, what do you think happens to the shell as the chick develops?

Exactly Eggs

Nate was excited about the unusual egg his hen laid. People often wonder how an egg develops inside a shell and hatches into a living creature. Below are some facts that might help you understand how an egg is produced from a chicken.

The Parts of the Egg

Shell: Composed of calcium carbonate, it is porous with about 7,000 holes. The pores (holes) permit the movement of gases through the shell. Beneath the shell are two thin membranes that keep the liquid of the egg from evaporating too quickly.

Air Space: When the egg is laid, it has the same body temperature as the hen—107 degrees Farenheit (41.6 degrees Celsius). The outside temperature is usually cooler, so the membrane inside shrinks, allowing an air pocket to form at one end of the shell. This air space is used by the chick on the 20th day of growth (incubation), when the chick pokes through the membrane and takes its first breath of air inside the shell.

Albumen: Otherwise known as "the white" of the egg, it has a large amount of protein for nutrition for the developing chick (embryo). The albumen is separated into a thick liquid and a thin liquid.

Chalazae (pronounced kə-la-zə): Two white twisted strands of fibers, it holds the yolk in place at the center of the egg.

Yolk: The yellow-orange substance in the center of the egg is full of vitamins, minerals, carbohydrates, fats, and protein.

Germ Spot: The white spot that sits on the yolk, it is where the embryo begins to develop.

Using the terms above, identify the main parts of a normal hen's egg in the drawing below.

It would be interesting to research how the development of eggs is the same and different in other creatures like turtles, snakes, alligators, etc. Take the time to look up some information on these other creatures and share it with your classmates.

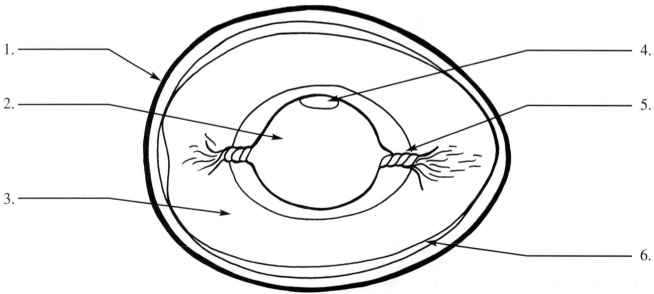

Your Own Story

Nate tells the story of *The Enormous Egg* in his own words. When a writer uses his own voice to tell a story it is referred to as writing in the first person.

Notice how Nate leads into the story by telling some background in the first chapter. "My name is Nate Twichell, but I can't help that." He tells a little about each person in his family before he begins to tell the story of the egg.

Using an interesting experience you have had, begin to tell about it in the first person, using "I" and the names of people who were connected to your experience. Use the outline below to guide you in the writing of your story in the first person.

Share a little bit about yourself and the characters in your story.

_____

_____

_____

_____

Describe what happened before the main event in your tale.

_____

_____

_____

_____

Explain in detail what happened to you. The more details you tell, the more alive the story will become.

_____

_____

_____

_____

How did your experience end? Why did you choose to write about it?

_____

_____

_____

_____

Share your story with the class after you have read it to one other person and listened to his or her response to your story. Rewrite some of it, if you need to, so people can better understand what you experienced.

Quiz Time!

Answer the following questions about Chapters 4–7 in complete sentences. You may use your book to find the answer.

1. What did the dinosaur look like when it hatched?

   _____

   _____

2. Why was Dr. Ziemer so excited when he heard that the egg had hatched?

   _____

   _____

3. What kind of doctor was Dr. Ziemer?

   _____

   _____

4. Why did the doctor say that "Now the trouble begins"?

   _____

   _____

5. Why didn't Joe Champigny agree that Nate had a dinosaur even after he had seen it?

   _____

   _____

6. Why does a dinosaur need to eat pebbles?

   _____

   _____

7. What was the big problem Nate began to realize about the dinosaur?

   _____

   _____

8. How did Dr. Ziemer say a chicken and a turtle are alike?

   _____

   _____

9. Why was the name Uncle Beasley chosen for the dinosaur?

   _____

   _____

10. Where would you keep an animal if you knew it would grow to be 20 feet long?

   _____

   _____

Dino Coloring Book

Nate and his friend Joe Champigny knew very little about dinosaurs. However, they knew that dinosaurs were supposed to be extinct. Sometimes when we learn a few facts about something we develop a new interest.

Creating a Coloring Book

One of the ways we can learn is through a coloring book. In the space provided, create a simple drawing that illustrates one or some of the dinosaurs listed below. Create the picture in a fashion that will allow a younger child to color it easily. Neatly print two interesting facts about that dinosaur under your picture. Use your library, books, magazines, or the computer to help you create your dinosaur page. Add details to the background as it might have existed then. When your sketch is done, carefully outline it with a thin, dark marker. Erase all pencil lines. Have your teacher make copies for the class to share, and later combine these into a booklet. Create a cover and give the booklet to a younger student.

- triceratops
- voelophysis
- edmontosaurus
- tyrannosaurus

- elaphrosaurus
- iguanodon
- stegosaurus
- allosaurus

- ornintholestes
- protoceratops
- barosaurus
- pachycephalosaurus

- spinosaurus
- diplodocus

Staple this side.

_____

_____

_____

Choices and Consequences

In *The Enormous Egg,* Nate made many choices that could have changed the situation for Uncle Beasley and him. Often we make decisions without considering the consequences. Below are a set of choices that Nate could have made. A set of consequences is also listed. With a partner, decide which consequence would go with each choice and write it in the space provided.

When the hen laid the huge egg, Nate could have . . .

Choices	Consequences
had the egg for breakfast.	
allowed the hen to take care of it herself.	
cared for it for 21 days and then opened it.	
brought it to the church to show off.	

When Nate knew the egg had hatched, he could have . . .

Choices	Consequences
not called Dr. Ziemer.	
tried to keep it.	
kept Uncle Beasley in his room.	

Possible Consequences

- Nate's parents would have been annoyed.
- It would grow too large for the space.
- He would not have known what to feed the baby dinosaur, and it would have died.
- He would have found the dinosaur embryo that would not be able to live.
- He got to taste it and save the shell.
- It might have dropped and broken or gotten chilled and not hatched.
- The hen might not have been able to turn it, and it would have died.

Call the Doctor!

When Dr. Ziemer told the Twichell family that he was a doctor of paleontology and not a medical doctor, they were surprised. When people earn a doctor's degree, called a Ph.D. or doctorate, it is for studying one type of knowledge. There are many types of doctors, and sometimes it can become confusing to tell them apart.

Directions: Below is a list of doctorate degrees. See if you can find out what each one does.

1. doctor of paleontology _____

2. doctor of anthropology _____

3. doctor of biology _____

4. doctor of microbiology _____

5. doctor of entomology _____

6. doctor of ornithology _____

7. doctor of botany _____

8. doctor of ichthyology _____

9. doctor of meteorology _____

10. doctor of zoology _____

Directions: See if you can tell which doctor you would go to in each situation below.

11. You would like to go into the woods and learn about the plants and animals living there. _____

    _____

12. There are strange things growing on the baseball glove you left out in the rain, and you want to know what they are. _____

13. A goose lands in your yard, and you want to know what kind it is. _____

14. Is the ancient arrowhead found in your yard authentic? _____

15. You want to know how people lived in the years before civilization. _____

16. What do shark eggs look like? _____

17. You are looking for the fastest animal in the world. _____

18. What is a plant that eats flies? _____

19. Where is the Big Dipper in the sky? _____

20. You find an unusual insect in your basement. Is it poisonous? _____

Being a Caretaker

Nate had to take on the responsibility of caring for Uncle Beasley. He had to gather lots of grass for food, walk Uncle Beasley, and keep him safe. Having a new pet can be a lot of responsibility but can also be a lot of fun.

- Take time to meet some new types of pets. You can go to a pet store or a zoo, or visit a friend who has an unusual pet. Ask questions about the animal that might help you learn how to take care of it.

- Use the library or the Internet to learn about interesting pets a person might have, like a frog, horse, deer, bird, snake, spider, pig, etc.

- List what you learned about caring for this unusual pet.

Below are some questions you should be able to answer based on your research.

- What kind of pet is it? _____

- What does it eat? Does it eat more than one thing?_____

- How often must you feed it? _____

- How do you keep it clean? How often do you clean it? _____

- What type of bed does it need in which to rest?_____

- Must you take it for walks? How often? _____

- How often must you clean up after it? _____

- What kind of training will it need so it can live well with you? How long will it take to do this?

  _____

- What can it learn to do?_____

- Must someone be with it all the time, or can it be on its own? _____

- Does it get lonely? Do you need to have more than one at a time? _____

- Does it need to be groomed? How often? _____

- What type of house should it have? _____

- What must you consider when having other people around it, for their safety and your pet's?

  _____

- What are some other interesting things you found out about your choice of a pet that you never knew about? _____

- If you could actually have this unusual animal as a pet, would you?_____

Quiz Time!

Answer the following questions about Chapters 8–11 in complete sentences. You may use your book to find the answers.

1. What made Dr. Kennedy think Dr. Ziemer was trying to fool him?

   _____

   _____

2. How much had Uncle Beasley grown in the first 24 hours?

   _____

   _____

3. Why do you think Nate wouldn't sell Uncle Beasley?

   _____

   _____

4. How was the Twichell household disrupted when the news got out that they had a dinosaur?

   _____

   _____

5. What was the name of Mr. Twichell's newspaper?

   _____

   _____

6. What kinds of offers did Nate get for his dinosaur?

   _____

   _____

7. How large is a triceratops expected to grow, and how much is it likely to weigh?

   _____

   _____

8. In what way was Nate responsible for Uncle Beasley?

   _____

   _____

9. How did they have to weigh Uncle Beasley since he had gotten so big?

   _____

   _____

10. What important decision did the Twichell family make about Nate and the dinosaur?

    _____

    _____

Biscuits for Breakfast

Several times in the book *The Enormous Egg* Mrs. Twichell made biscuits for breakfast. Below is a recipe for biscuits that you might like to prepare.

Make sure you gather all of the ingredients before you begin to prepare the recipe.

Applesauce Cheese Biscuits

Utensils

- measuring spoon and cup
- oven
- mixing bowls
- large spoon to mix
- cookie sheet
- rolling pin
- round cookie cutter
- 2 butter knives for cutting dough or a pastry blender
- board or table to roll out dough
- paper towels

Ingredients

- 2 cups (480 mL) all-purpose flour
- 2 teaspoons (10 mL) baking powder
- ¼ teaspoon (1.25 mL) baking soda
- 1 teaspoon (5 mL) salt
- ¼ cup (60 mL) vegetable shortening
- ¾ cup (180 mL) applesauce
- ¾ cup (180 mL) grated sharp cheddar cheese

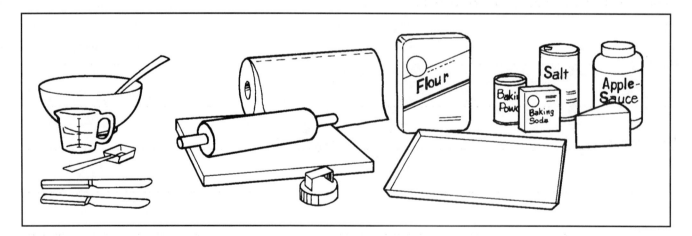

Cooking Instructions

Preheat the oven to 400°F (200°C). Mix the flour, baking powder, baking soda, and salt. Cut in the shortening with the two knives or pastry blender. Mix in the applesauce and cheese. Roll out dough so it is ½ inch (1.3 cm) thick. If it sticks to the surface, dust it with a small amount of flour. Cut dough into two-inch rounds and place on ungreased baking sheet. Bake for 8–10 minutes or until the biscuits are lightly browned. Allow to cool on a paper towel before eating. May be enjoyed with butter or jam and a glass of milk.

Perhaps your class could plan a special breakfast together and invite another grade or class to be your guests. Discuss what you would include in the breakfast to make it welcoming, delicious, and healthful.

You're Like That!

Everyone has a different personality. Nate, Joe Champigny, Mr. and Mrs. Twichell, and Cynthia all had different personality traits. Below is a list of characters in *The Enormous Egg*. Working with a partner, match the characters with the traits that seem reasonable to you. Share the results with your classmates.

Nate	Dr. Kennedy	Mrs. Twichell	Captain Neeley
Dr. Ziemer	Joe Champigny	Mr. Twichell	Cynthia

1. decisive _____

2. skeptical _____

3. reasonable _____

4. reliable _____

5. impatient _____

6. curious _____

7. hardworking _____

8. excitable _____

After completing this exercise, try to compare people you know with these personality traits. Explain to your partner why you made these matches.

curious_____

_____

hardworking _____

_____

reliable_____

_____

excitable _____

_____

decisive _____

_____

Place the Dinosaur

Scientists like Dr. Ziemer have studied the remains of dinosaurs found buried in the earth or even frozen in ice. By testing the bones and studying the layers in which bones were found, paleontologists have been able to place specific dinosaurs in specific periods of time. Below are a few paragraphs giving you some information about these fascinating creatures.

Giants of the Earth

Dinosaurs appeared on the earth about 225 million years ago in a period of time called the Triassic Period. Desert conditions existed with only some areas of shallow water. The vegetation consisted of tree ferns and conifers. Dinosaurs were reptiles living on the land. The gliding, swimming, and flying reptiles such as the Pteranodon were not considered dinosaurs. There were crocodile-like animals. These animals all had strong hind legs and long tails. Some animals walked on hind legs and used their tails for balance. They were named the Thecodonts of the Triassic Period. Some of the Thecodonts were: Rutiodon, Coelophysis, and Plateosaurus. This period lasted until 208 million years ago.

The second period of time was the Jurassic Period. It lasted from 208 to 146 million years ago. The land separated from the shallow seas and the climate was moist. The land was covered with ferns, conifers, and cycads. The plant eaters had grown huge, and some had developed armor for protection from the meat eaters. The long-necked plant eaters were the largest animals that ever lived. The skies were filled with flying reptiles, and many of the land animals had become four-footed. Some of the largest animals of this period were Heterodontosaurus, Stegosaurus, and Dilophosaurus.

The Cretaceous Period was the third period of the dinosaur life on earth, from 146 million years ago to 65 million years ago. During this time some of the lands dried out, and most of the habitable climates were on the coast. As time progressed, plant life became more like what we have today. There were long-necked plant eaters, large and small meat eaters, and armored and horned dinosaurs. Just when dinosaurs were at their largest and most interesting, for some reason they died out, and only the smaller, related creatures remained. Some of the creatures from the Cretaceous Period were Tyrannosaurus and Triceratops.

Write the correct time period below each dinosaur on the line provided.

1. _____

2. _____

3. _____

4. _____

5. _____

6. _____

To Go Where You Have Never Gone Before

Dr. Kennedy had a hard time finding the Twichell home in Freedom, New Hampshire, because he had little experience getting around in the country. Often when we experience something new, we are uncomfortable. However, a new situation often opens the door to learn many new things.

Below are some places you may never have had the chance to experience before. Arrange with your teacher, parents, or a responsible adult to take a field trip to one of the places listed below. You can also brainstorm with your classmates other places you might enjoy visiting for the first time.

- a local museum
- a farm that raises livestock
- a horse ranch
- a subway station
- a pig farm
- a kitchen in a big restaurant
- a dog or cat show
- an opera
- a barn dance
- a factory
- an artist's studio
- a boatyard
- a police station

Write about your experience in the space provided and share it with your classmates. Include where you went, the people you met, what happened there, and an event you found interesting.

_____

_____

_____

_____

_____

_____

_____

_____

Quiz Time!

Answer the following questions about Chapters 12–14 in complete sentences. You may use your book to find the answers.

1. Where did they take Uncle Beasley in Washington?

    _____

    _____

2. How did Nate continue his schoolwork while he was in Washington?

    _____

    _____

3. What caused the accident when Uncle Beasley and Nate were out walking?

    _____

    _____

4. What did the police captain say about Uncle Beasley?

    _____

    _____

5. Where did they take Uncle Beasley after he left the Washington National Museum?

    _____

    _____

6. Why might Uncle Beasley being in the zoo be a problem?

    _____

    _____

7. How would a congressman's opinion affect the animals in the zoo?

    _____

    _____

8. Why might the zoo be a good place for Uncle Beasley?

    _____

    _____

9. Why were there no elephants in the zoo?

    _____

    _____

10. What do you think might become the next problem for Nate and Uncle Beasley?

    _____

    _____

Be the Scientist

Dr. Ziemer was a paleontologist: a scientist who studies fossils of animals and plants from the past. He could take the skeleton of an animal and create an image of what it would look like when it was alive.

Below are the skeletons of common animals.

You be the scientist and draw what you think they looked like when they were alive. What animals do you think they were? Write your guesses on the line below each skeleton.

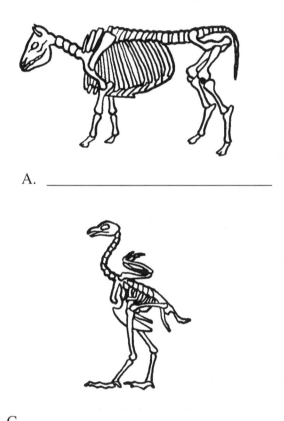

A. _____

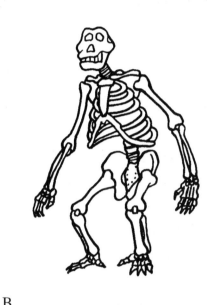

B. _____

C. _____

D. _____

E. _____

A World of Schooling

Nate was allowed to go to Washington with Uncle Beasley as long as he kept up with his schoolwork. There are places where you can learn besides school. With a friend, look at the school subjects below. Decide where (other than the classroom) you can learn about the subject and what you need to know about it to get along in the world.

Where or to whom would you go to learn more about . . .?

Math

money _____

measuring_____

figuring (adding, subtracting, etc.) _____

English

speaking correctly _____

writing _____

handwriting _____

reading _____

Social Studies

history _____

geography _____

civics (study of government)_____

computers_____

Other Areas of Study

physical education _____

music _____

Share this information with the class when you have completed the list.

On a separate sheet of paper, list other ideas you or your classmates may have about learning in the world.

Freedom, New Hampshire, to Washington, D.C.

Uncle Beasley and Nate made the trip from Freedom, New Hampshire, to Washington, D.C., in one day's travel. Trace their route on the map below and answer some questions about their trip.

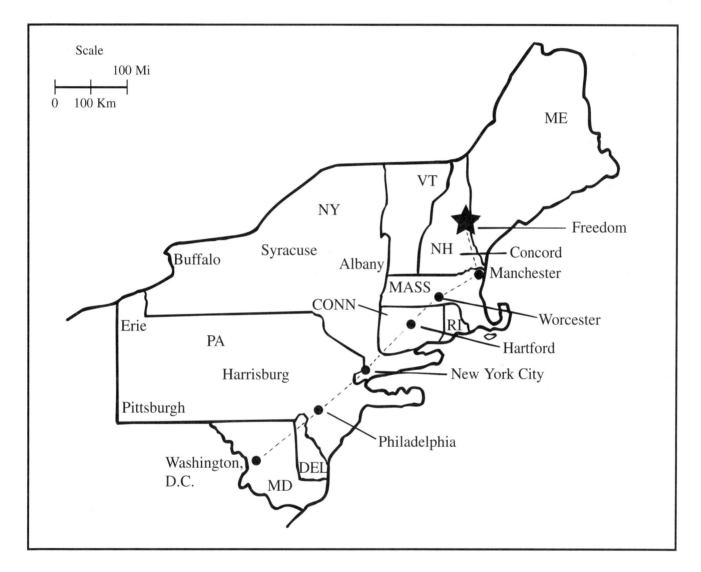

Find the distance they traveled, using the scale shown above the map. _____

Using a calculator, find the driving time if they drove at 65 miles per hour the entire way. _____

Name the states through which they traveled. _____

Since they left at 6:30 in the morning, what time do you think they arrived in Washington, D.C.?

_____

Planning a Trip

Dr. Ziemer helped plan the trip for Uncle Beasley and Nate from Freedom, New Hampshire, to Washington, D.C. It was a long trip, but they never got lost because they had planned well. Try your luck at planning a trip from your hometown to someplace you would like to visit. Get a map of your state, and use a light-colored marker to trace the roads you would travel to get to your destination.

Below are some items you might want to consider.

Travel Itinerary

From _____ to _____

Roads over which you will travel: _____

_____

Distance traveled from home: _____

Time to drive distance: _____

What time will you leave home? _____

What time will you reach your destination? _____

What meals will you need to take with you? _____

_____

What will you do in the car to keep yourself amused for the time it takes to travel?

_____

What will you pass as you travel that will be interesting to see? _____

_____

_____

What will you see when you get there? _____

_____

_____

Share with the class, create a bulletin board, or make a display of your adventure.

Quiz Time!

Answer the following questions about Chapters 15–17 in complete sentences. You may use your book to find the answers.

1. Senator Granderson asked Dr. Ziemer what good a triceratops was. Why is that a hard question to answer?

_____

_____

2. What reason did Senator Granderson give for not wanting to keep the dinosaur?

_____

_____

3. What did the Senator suggest be done with Uncle Beasley?

_____

_____

4. What idea did Dr. Ziemer think would save Uncle Beasley?

_____

_____

5. Why didn't Dr. Ziemer want Nate to read the speech they wrote for him?

_____

_____

6. How did the public respond to Nate's talk on TV?

_____

_____

7. What do you think happened to the dinosaur bill?

_____

_____

8. What gift did Dr. Ziemer give to Nate?

_____

_____

9. How was Nate greeted when he finally came home?

_____

_____

10. Do you feel that Mr. Twichell's suggestion for Nate to write down his story was a good suggestion? Explain why or why not.

_____

_____

Passing a Bill

In *The Enormous Egg,* Senator Granderson was elected to make laws for the people who elected him. The bill he was proposing to make into a law would affect Uncle Beasley.

To see a bill become a law, use your classroom and classmates to reenact the passage of a law.

❏ Choose one person in your room to be president. Choose five to be senators and ten to be members of the House of Representatives. (If the class is not large enough, enlist the help of another class.)

❏ Choose one of the ideas below for the bill you would like to make into a law, or decide on your own idea.

Ideas for Bills

1. All students in your grade must use one recess a month to help first graders with their homework.

2. Parents are to sign all homework papers.

3. All children under four feet tall are to be first in line for everything.

4. The class is to spend 5 minutes of each day singing.

5. Students must e-mail their teacher each evening when homework is complete.

6. Students who do not do well in a subject must spend time in a lower grade studying that subject.

❏ Have senators and representatives discuss why they might vote for the bill and why they might not. If taking turns speaking becomes a problem, have a speaking hat or stick to pass around. The remainder of the class are citizens, whose job is to convince their congressperson with letters and personal conversations.

❏ When discussions are done, the vote is taken. If the bill passes in each body of Congress, the president decides if he or she will sign the bill into law.

❏ If someone complains, the teacher, who is not elected, will be the judge and declare whether the new law is fair.

❏ If the bill is not passed, try another bill.

How Congress Does It

Understanding how Congress passes a bill into a law helped Dr. Ziemer and Nate to save Uncle Beasley. Below is a chart showing how a law is passed in the United States. Using the key words at the bottom of the chart, fill in the blanks for the process of turning a bill into a law.

Word Bank

Senate	Congress	representatives
senators	executive	judicial
House of Representatives		

A bill can be proposed by _____,

or the _____. Then it is sent to

the _____ . And if passed here,

it is sent to the_____. If the bill

passes both bodies of _____, it is

sent to the _____branch. If the

president signs it, then it becomes a law. If a

citizen thinks it's an unfair law, he or she

may take it to the _____

branch of the government where it can be

declared fair or unfair (unconstitutional). If it

is unconstitutional, it will no longer be a law.

Speech! Speech!

Nate had to make a speech in front of a TV camera to try to help Uncle Beasley. A speech had been written for him, but he was not happy with it because it did not say what he felt. When he used his own words, his argument convinced people to help Uncle Beasley.

With a partner choose a subject about which you both feel strongly, and prepare a three-minute speech for your class. You may videotape it for a TV or computer or present it to your class in person.

Some suggestions to get you thinking are listed below:

- Older students should spend time helping younger students.
- Recess should be at the end of the day before the students go home.
- Parents should get paid for the work they do at home.
- Students in school should buy their own books.
- School children should wear uniforms.
- All schools should require dance lessons.
- Students who do not complete homework should pay a fine.
- Students who fight should be in a separate class.
- Schools should offer special art and music classes on Saturday.

While you are presenting your speech, look up at the audience as much as possible. Practice your speech at least four times and make sure it fits into three minutes.

The following are some ways to get ready for your speech:

1. Have an interesting beginning to get the attention of the class.
2. State your main idea in one sentence.
3. Give the reasons why you support your main idea.
4. Tell how it would be better if everyone agreed with you.
5. Explain how your proposed idea (what you think is right) can be done.
6. Repeat your main idea at the end and thank your audience for listening.

A Political Letter

Nate went to visit Senator Granderson to talk about Uncle Beasley. You may want to do the same thing if you feel strongly about an issue. However, if you aren't able to meet with someone, write a letter, call on the phone, or send an e-mail.

Think about something you would like to suggest or find out about, and write a letter to your mayor, congressperson, or even the president. Check the blue pages of your phone book for listings and addresses of people whom you might want to contact.

State your purpose for writing, give examples to support your point of view, and don't forget to thank the person who has taken the time to read your letter.

Work with your teacher in organizing your letter in the correct form. Write as neatly as you can or type your letter.

Use the example below as a model for your letter. Write your own letter on a separate sheet of paper after reading the sample.

> Big Valley School
> 146 School Way
> Tenten, NY 18721
>
> March 16, 2000
>
> Dear Mr. President,
>
> I am a member of our school band. I am writing to ask you to give attention to children who have so little money that they cannot buy instruments to be in the band. This isn't fair. Some students I know are very talented but cannot join the band because their parents don't have enough money. Music is very important in life. Maybe the students can work at the school to help pay for their instruments, or the school can have a special collection for them. The government could even have a special fund so people can donate old instruments for them to borrow. Please try to solve this problem soon. Thank you for your time.
>
> Sincerely,
>
> Tom Strongnote

Any Questions?

When you finished reading *The Enormous Egg,* did you have some unanswered questions? Write them here.

_____

_____

_____

_____

_____

_____

_____

_____

Work together in a group to prepare possible answers for some or all of the questions you have asked above and those written below. When you have finished, share your ideas with the class.

- What made Nate decide to take on the responsibility of caring for the unusual egg he found?

- What will become of Uncle Beasley at the National Zoo?

- Do you think the town of Freedom, New Hampshire, will remain famous in the future?

- Will Nate continue to go to Washington, D.C. to visit Uncle Beasley, and will Uncle Beasley remember him?

- Do you think Nate will regret not having sold the dinosaur for a lot of money when he had the chance?

- Do you think things would have turned out differently if the Twichell family had taken a different attitude toward the egg or the dinosaur?

- What might have happened if Nate had taken his dinosaur on a tour around the world or just traveled around the United States with Uncle Beasley? Write down some possible outcomes and share them with your classmates.

- Do you think that Nate's relationship with Dr. Ziemer will continue through the years?

- What do you think Cynthia will become as she grows up because of her experience with the dinosaur egg in her family?

- What do you think Nate will become when he grows up? Could his experience with Dr. Ziemer and Uncle Beasley affect his decision?

Book Report Ideas

There are many ways to tell about a story you have just read. After you have completed reading *The Enormous Egg*, choose an interesting way of reporting your story. It may be through an idea of your own, a teacher's suggestion, or one of the ideas below.

Roll the Film

Make a list of scenes in the story that are interesting. In a size-appropriate group, dress up and pose for the scenes you have chosen. Have a parent or another student take pictures of your scenes. Have them developed and display them in order on a poster with comments under each picture telling what was happening in the photo.

Interview

Set up two chairs in front of the room, as though you were being interviewed. Choose a friend to be the interviewer. Have the questions ready ahead of time for the interviewer to ask you. Speak as though you are one of the characters in the story as you answer the interviewer's questions. Make it interesting by developing an accent or some mannerisms that you think the character in the story might have.

Flashlight Show

Create large drawings, at least 22" x 17" (56 cm x 43 cm), of six main parts of the story. Put the drawings on the board in order. Darken the room and tell the story while shining a flashlight on the poster that illustrates the part of the story you are explaining.

Kiddy Book

Think of the picture books you have read. Using large white paper and the type of coloring tool you choose, create a picture book telling the story of *The Enormous Egg* in simple terms that a young child could read. Read your book with a younger student and donate it to that class' library.

Order! Order!

Using 14 cards, place one letter of the title, *The Enormous Egg*, on each card. Keeping the cards in order, turn them over and write parts of the story, in order, on the back of each card. Distribute the cards to the class and ask the students to form a line so that their cards spell out the title of the book. It might be good to combine some of the double letters to ease confusion, for example, "En" and "Eg." Once students are in order, have them read the summary in the order in which they are standing.

Reader's Sentinel

As a group project, each student writes a summary of an assigned chapter or section of the book. Using a computer if possible, type in 4-inch (10 cm) columns. Print and cut them to fit in a newspaper format. Use *who, what, when, where, why,* and *how* information in each of the summaries. Arrange the "newspaper" together with a header, headlines, and bylines. Make copies to take home or to give to another class.

Scavenger Hunt

Nate learned a great deal studying at the National Museum. Working in teams and with a time limit, answer as many questions on this scavenger hunt as you can. Use books from the library and your computer to research the questions below. Work on them in any order. Write your answers on a separate sheet of paper.

1. Why did some dinosaurs have eyes on the sides of their heads while others had eyes in the front?

2. What was the tallest plant-eating dinosaur?

3. Which dinosaur had belly armor, a lesothosaurus or a minmi?

4. What did a dinosaur nest look like?

5. What was the size of a maiasaur's eggs?

6. How many toes did a tyrannosaurus have on each of its front feet?

7. What dinosaur had two rows of protective plates down its back?

8. What modern bird does the gallimimus resemble?

9. What crime did the oviraptor commit?

10. What did the archaeopteryx have that modern birds do not?

11. What was unusual about the megalosaurus' teeth?

12. Was allosaurus a plant eater or a meat eater?

13. How long was the mamenchesaurus' neck?

14. What did parasaurolophus have that made it look very unusual?

15. What did the triceratops use its horns for?

16. What was the smallest dinosaur (only two feet long)?

17. What does the psaittacosaurus have in common with a parrot?

18. What is the shell of a dinosaur egg like?

19. How many types of dinosaurs were there?

20. What is unusual about Crystal Park in London, England?

Accordion Booklet

Many interesting events happened in *The Enormous Egg*. One of the ways to remember these events is to record them with a drawing in an accordion booklet. Working with a partner, discuss the major events in several or all of the chapters in the book. Using the booklet below, draw and color the main event in each of the chapters. Indicate the chapter number you are illustrating and use short titles to explain your artwork.

When your drawing is complete, cut out the strips and tape them together. Carefully fold the booklet back and forth accordion style along the dotted lines.

The Enormous Egg

by

Oliver Butterworth

Chapter _____

Chapter _____

_____

_____

Chapter _____

Chapter _____

Chapter _____

_____

_____

_____

Point of View

A point of view can change how a situation appears. In *The Enormous Egg,* the story is written from Nate's point of view. Try choosing one of the characters in the story and telling it from that character's point of view. Place the character's name in the space below and tell the story using the first person "I." Share and describe with your class how the story takes on a different feel when told from another point of view.

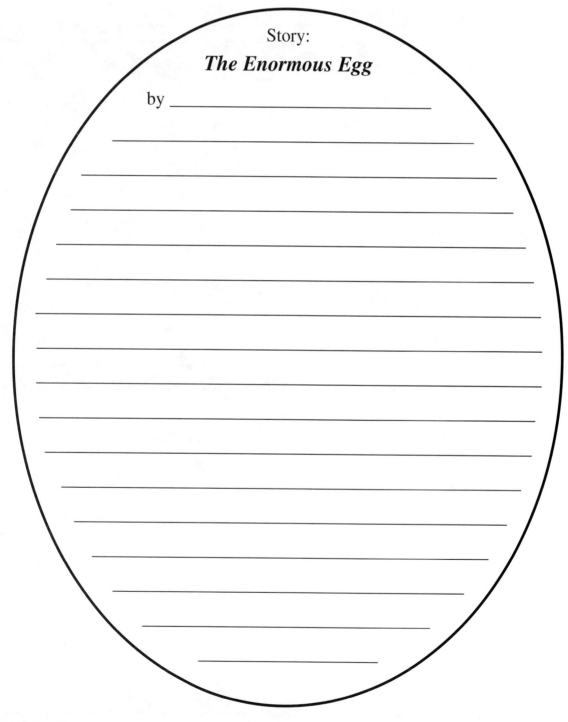

Story:
The Enormous Egg

by _____

Dino Game Board

The Twichell family learned many new things when they decided to take care of the unusual egg. Perhaps it would be fun to make and play a game using some of the facts you have learned from reading *The Enormous Egg*.

Below is a suggestion of how your class can construct their own Dino Game. As a cooperative class effort, students can complete various portions of the project.

Materials

- 2 pieces of flat cardboard—21" x 30" (53 cm x 76 cm)
- box for storing cards and pieces for play
- dice or pair of small boxes covered with paper and marked with numbers on each side
- markers or colored pencils
- white paper for squares on board
- clear contact paper or laminate
- spools for playing pieces (or any usable material)
- bookbinding tape (or any strong tape)

Directions

1. In pencil, mark off 3-inch (8 cm) squares on three sides of each board. (See diagram.)

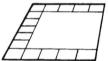

2. Cut out 20 three-inch (8 cm) squares of white paper. Print the directions for turns clearly, including a Start and End space and six Choose Card squares. Color squares so they can be easily read.

 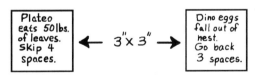

3. Plan where to place squares and glue them down.

4. Cut white paper for the center of each board and decorate. Paste half on each board as shown in the diagram.

Dino Game Board *(cont.)*

5. Laminate both sides of the game board separately.

6. Tape the center of the boards together with bookbinding tape, leaving a small space between the boards for folding.

7. Create 20 game cards 1½" x 3" (3.8 cm x 8 cm). Write true or false facts about dinosaurs on these cards. Whenever a player draws a card and he or she determines correctly that the fact is true or false, the player moves an additional space on the board. If the player answers incorrectly, the player moves back one step. Write the answer for each fact on the bottom right corner of each card.

8. Play the game.

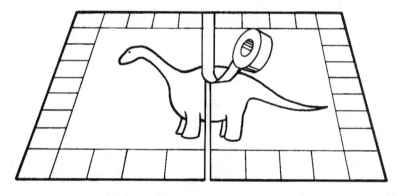

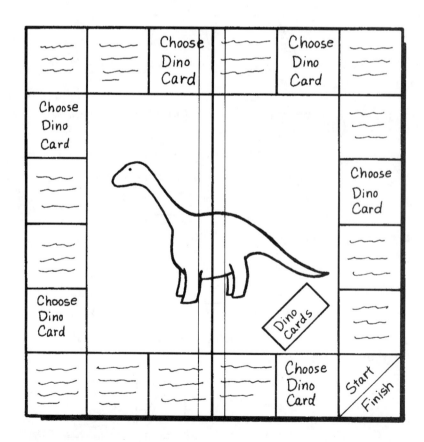

Objective and Essay Test

Matching: Match the quote with the person who said it.

Nate	Mother	Joe Champigny
Cynthia	Dr. Ziemer	Senator Granderson
Pop	Dr. Kennedy	Mr. Bonelli

1. _____ "But just remember, if it's a crocodile or a dragon or something like that, I won't have it in my house for one minute."

2. _____ "Believe it or not, you people have hatched out a dinosaur."

3. _____ "He's just making fun of you. These summer people think they're awful smart, and they think that just because we live up here in Freedom, New Hampshire, we don't know anything. They think we're all suckers for jokes like this. That's what my dad says."

4. _____ "How about it, boy? We can give you a hundred dollars for your animal, right as it stands. You wouldn't want to turn down an offer like that, would you? How about it?"

5. _____ "I know something you don't know—it's something about you. I heard Dr. Ziemer talking to Mom and Pop about it this afternoon."

6. _____ "We must not maintain foreign freaks at the public's expense. Lions, tigers, giraffes—all the proper animals, yes. But no un-American, outmoded creatures from foreign places. The dinosaurs are extinct, aren't they? Do you want people to get the false idea that such things still exist, right here in America?"

7. _____ "Why in—in the name of goodness didn't you read the speech I gave you?"

8. _____ "I'm not going to do anything with him—I just want to have him. Isn't it enough just to have something?"

9. _____ "We could all have it for breakfast—how many minutes would you boil an egg that size?"

True or False: Write true or false next to each statement below.

1. _____ Nate was looking to sell the dinosaur for as much as he could get.

2. _____ Nate had to do schoolwork when he was in Washington.

3. _____ The people of Freedom were angry because Nate had given the dinosaur away.

4. _____ Dr. Ziemer was trying to get Nate to give up the dinosaur.

5. _____ The dinosaur took walks around the city of Washington with Nate.

Sequence: Number the events below in the order they occurred in the story.

_____ The dinosaur is sent to the Washington Zoo.

_____ Nate goes on television to ask people for help.

_____ The hen had laid a very unusual and large egg.

_____ Senator Granderson tries to get rid of Uncle Beasley.

Paragraphs: On the back of this sheet, answer these questions in paragraphs.

1. Discuss what you feel was the reason Nate might have had for spending so much time and energy on the egg and the dinosaur once it was hatched. How can this relate to your life?

2. Discuss how you felt the members of the Twichell family were supportive of each other. What were some of the problems that might have occured if they hadn't been so supportive?

Responses

Explain the meaning of each of these quotations from *The Enormous Egg*. Choose as many of the quotations as seems reasonable.

Chapter 1: "If we did that sort of thing up here in Freedom, it would be a bad example to the rest of the country."

Chapter 2: "Now, Nate—you deserve a lot of credit for keeping at this thing the way you have. Just don't try to follow a lost cause farther than it's worth, will you?"

Chapter 4: "After all, if you've taken care of something for all that time you don't feel too much like joking about it."

Chapter 4: "Never mind that—there's no reason to give up going to church just because we've got a dinosaur out back."

Chapter 7: "That's why they are alike in some ways. How is a chicken like a turtle, for example?"

Chapter 8: "My land, Nate, how you talk! I didn't know you meant a toy animal. I thought you were looking for a live one. Why, hear the boy talk! I'm looking for a small dinosaur, he says."

Chapter 9: "I guess you'd better give it up, Kennedy. The scientists will just have to come up here to Freedom, whether they like it or not."

Chapter 9: "The idea, supper at almost eight o'clock. I don't see why everyone has to get in such a state over a little animal like that, even if it is a dinosaur."

Chapter 10: "Nate, if he goes along at this rate much longer, we're gong to have a problem on our hands."

Chapter 11: "You see, dinosaurs are reptiles, and they're not built for very cold weather. You know what turtles do in the winter, don't you?"

Chapter 11: "Boy am I lucky! I must be dreaming or something!"

Chapter 13: "We had expected something like that sooner or later—that dinosaur really isn't built to fit into modern traffic conditions."

Chapter 14: "Did you hear that, Ed? That's where the money goes.'"

Chapter 15: "You can call it anything you like, but the point is, what good is it?"

Chapter 15: "It isn't your fault, Dr. Ziemer, you were trying to do the best thing you could for him. You didn't know things would turn out this way."

Chapter 15: "—this animal I speak of is no normal creature like the lions and tigers and elephants that roam the woods and plains of our fair country."

Chapter 16: "And remember, it may be our only chance to save Uncle Beasley."

Chapter 16: "I guess they don't get excited about a thing until somebody starts taking it away from them."

Conversations

Work in size-appropriate groups to write and perform the conversations that might have occurred in each of the situations listed below.

- ❏ Nate tries to convince Joe Champigny that Uncle Beasley is really a dinosaur. (two people)

- ❏ An owner of a gas station tries to convince Nate that it is a good idea to sell or rent Uncle Beasley to him to help sell gas. (two people)

- ❏ The family and Dr. Ziemer sit at the supper table to make a decision about whether or not to keep Uncle Beasley. (five people)

- ❏ Senator Granderson tries to convince two other senators that they should ban dinosaurs in the United States. (three people)

- ❏ Ten years later, Nate tells a new story to a reporter about what has happened to Uncle Beasley in the past ten years. (two people)

- ❏ A scientist tries to explain to Nate how a dinosaur egg might come from a hen. (two people)

- ❏ Cynthia calls a friend on the phone and tries to explain what has happened at the hen house this summer. (two people)

- ❏ Nate tries to convince a police officer to let him take Uncle Beasley on a walk in the city. (two people)

- ❏ Cynthia and Nate decide that they want to keep Uncle Beasley. They try to convince their parents that they are able to take care of him. (four people)

Before you perform for the class, get together with your group and write out your parts in conversation form, making a separate copy of the script for each actor's part.

_____

_____

_____

_____

_____

_____

_____

_____

Bibliography of Related Reading

Dinosaurs

Barish, Wendy. *The Dinosaur Encyclopedia.* S & S Children, 1984.

Brett-Surman, Michael and Thomas Holtz. *The World of Dinosaurs: A North American Selection.* Greenwich Workshop, 1998.

Elridgc, Niles. *Fossil Factory: A Kid's Guide to Digging Up Dinosaurs, Exploring Evolution and Finding Fossils.* Addison-Wesley, 1989.

Esslinger, Jessica. *Discover Dinosaurs.* Roberts Rinehart, 1994.

Farlow, James O. *On the Tracks of Dinosaurs: A Study of Dinosaur Footprints.* Watts, 1991.

Gibbons, Tony. *Coelophysis: A Dinosaur from the Triassic Period.* Brown, 1994.

Gibbons, Tony. *Pterodactyls: A Dinosaur from the Jurassic Period.* Brown, 1994.

Gibbons, Tony. *Triceratops: A Dinosaur from the Cretaceous Period.* Brown, 1993.

Glut, Donald F. *The Age of Dinosaurs: A Fact-Filled Coloring Book.* Running Press, 1994.

Hall, Nancy. *Dinosaur Facts.* Random, 1998.

Hawcock, David. *Dinosaurs: Giants of the Earth.* Highlights, 1992.

Horner, Jack and Don Lessem. *Digging Up Tyrannosaurus Rex.* Crown Books, 1995.

Fiction Books

Delancy, M. C. *Henry's Special Delivery.* Dutton, 1984.

Fonham, Frank. *The Friends of the Loony Lake Monster.* Dutton, 1972.

Norton, Mary. *The Borrowers.* Harcourt, Brace, Jovanovich, 1952.

Seidler, Tor. *The Tat Pit.* Farrar, 1987.

Sloan, Carolyn. *The Sea Child.* Holiday, 1988.

Stiles, Ruth. *My Father's Dragon.* Random House, 1948.

On the Web

Bottle Cap Bones

http://www.pack-ofun.com/projects/capbones.htm

Dinosaurs Valley Museum

http://www.mwc.mus.co.us/dinosaurs/

Dinosaurs in Cyberspace: Dinolinks

http://www.ucmp.berkley.edu/diabsids/dinolinks.html

Answer Key

Page 11

1. The egg came from Nate's hen.
2. Accept appropriate responses.
3. He stayed in the basement so he would not bother the neighbors.
4. They kept their goat in her yard and wanted to continue to do so.
5. Accept appropriate responses.
6. The hen, Nate, and his dad took on the responsibility of turning the egg.
7. Accept appropriate responses.
8. Dr. Ziemer met Nate while they were both fishing.
9. Accept appropriate responses.
10. Accept appropriate responses.

Page 14

1. shell
2. yolk
3. albumen
4. germ spot
5. chalazae
6. air space

Page 16

1. It had three knobs sticking out of its head and a collar over its neck.
2. He knew it was something very unusual.
3. Dr. Ziemer was a paleontologist.
4. People would start to come from all over to see the dinosaur.
5. Accept appropriate responses.
6. The pebbles help to digest food.
7. Nate realized that he would need a great amount of grass to feed him.
8. They both lay eggs and have scaly skin.
9. Nate's Great-Uncle Beasley looked like him.
10. Accept appropriate responses.

Page 19

1. prehistoric animals or geologic times
2. origins of humans
3. living organisms and life processes
4. microorganisms

5. insects
6. birds
7. plants
8. fish
9. weather and weather conditions
10. animals
11. biology
12. microbiology
13. ornithology
14. paleontology
15. anthropology
16. ichthyology
17. zoology
18. botany
19. meteorology
20. entomology

Page 21

1. Dr. Kennedy didn't believe that dinosaurs lived today, and when he went to look in the box, there was nothing there.
2. He had doubled his weight.
3. Accept appropriate responses.
4. Accept appropriate responses.
5. The newspaper was the *Freedom Sentinel*.
6. The offers were for an advertisement for a gas station, a whiskey company, and a luggage company.
7. Triceratops could grow to twenty feet and weigh ten tons.
8. Nate fed him and walked him.
9. They weighed him on two scales on a board in the feed mill.
10. Nate and Uncle Beasley were going to Washington.

Page 23

1. Captain Neeley
2. Joe Champigny
3. Mr. Twichell
4. Nate
5. Dr. Kennedy
6. Dr. Ziemer
7. Mrs. Twichell
8. Cynthia

Answer Key *(cont.)*

Page 24

1. Jurrasic
2. Cretaceous
3. Triassic
4. Cretaceous
5. Cretaceous
6. Triassic

Page 26

1. They took him to the Washington National Museum.
2. He did his schoolwork at the museum.
3. The driver blew his horn.
4. They couldn't keep Uncle Beasley there.
5. They took him to the National Zoological Park.
6. It cost too much to feed him.
7. Accept appropriate responses.
8. Accept appropriate responses.
9. They cost too much to feed.
10. Accept appropriate responses.

Page 27

A. Cow
B. Gorilla
C. Chicken
D. Fish
E. Lizard

Page 29

Answers will vary. Accept all appropriate responses.

Page 31

1. Accept appropriate responses.
2. It was un-American.
3. He wanted to exterminate the dinosaur.
4. Nate should go on TV.
5. Accept appropriate responses.
6. They sent telegrams, came to the zoo, and donated money.
7. The senators changed their minds, and the bill was not passed.
8. He gave Nate a fossil dinosaur egg.
9. They had a parade for him.
10. Accept appropriate responses.

Page 33

Senators or representatives (order may vary), House of Representatives, Senate, Congress, executive, judicial

Page 38

Scavenger Hunt

1. The meat eaters had eyes forward to help them pursue food (prey), and the plant eaters had eyes on the side to be aware of what is behind them or chasing them.
2. barosaurus
3. minmi
4. hollowed-out mounds of earth
5. the size of a human head
6. two
7. stegosaurus
8. ostrich
9. stealing and eating
10. teeth
11. New ones grew when old ones were lost.
12. meat eater
13. 50 ft. (15 m)
14. a long crest on its head
15. to defend itself against the meat eaters
16. compsognathus
17. They both have beaks.
18. leathery
19. 900 to 1,200
20. a park with models of dinosaurs

Page 43

Matching

1. Mother
2. Dr. Ziemer
3. Joe Champigny
4. Dr. Kennedy
5. Cynthia
6. Senator Granderson
7. Mr. Bonelli
8. Nate
9. Pop

True or False

1. False
2. True
3. False
4. False
5. True

Sequence: 2-4-1-3

Paragraphs: Accept appropriate responses.